How Is Root Beer Made?

by Grace Hansen

Abdo
HOW IS IT MADE?
Kids

Abdo Kids Jumbo is an Imprint of Abdo Kids
abdobooks.com

abdobooks.com

Published by Abdo Kids, a division of ABDO, P.O. Box 398166, Minneapolis, Minnesota 55439.

102018

012019

THIS BOOK CONTAINS
RECYCLED MATERIALS

Photo Credits: Alamy, AP Images, Getty Images, iStock, Shutterstock, ©Pymouss p.9/CC-BY-SA-3.0

Production Contributors: Teddy Borth, Jennie Forsberg, Grace Hansen

Design Contributors: Dorothy Toth, Laura Mitchell

Library of Congress Control Number: 2018945980

Publisher's Cataloging-in-Publication Data

Names: Hansen, Grace, author.

Title: How is root beer made? / by Grace Hansen.

Description: Minneapolis, Minnesota : Abdo Kids, 2019 | Series: How is it made?
Includes glossary, index and online resources (page 24).

Identifiers: ISBN 9781532181962 (lib. bdg.) | ISBN 9781532182945 (ebook) |
ISBN 9781532183430 (Read-to-me ebook)

Subjects: LCSH: Soft drinks--Juvenile literature. | Manufacturing processes--
Juvenile literature. | Carbonated beverages--Juvenile literature.

Classification: DDC 663.6--dc23

Table of Contents

Root Tea to Root Beer

Root teas have been around for centuries. Root beer as we know it wasn't bottled until 1886. A **pharmacist** named Charles Elmer Hires began bottling his root tea **extract**.

Hires
SINCE 1876
ROOT BEER
WITH ROOTS-BARKS-HERBS

Edward Barq began bottling his root beer in 1898. People loved its sharp taste. Hires and Barq's Root Beer are still sold today!

The Original ROOT BEER
STAND

Common Flavors

The first step in making root beer is to **steep** the flavors. Sassafras flavor is key to making root beer. Other common flavors include vanilla, wintergreen, and many more.

The flavors are combined with water and sugar. Large cola companies make root beer with high fructose corn syrup. Serious root beer **brewers** use sweeteners like pure cane sugar.

Brewing the Brew

The mixture is brought to a boil. Then it is brought to a simmer for at least 30 minutes.

13

The ingredients are then **filtered** out, leaving a tasty liquid!

Once it has cooled enough, **yeast** is added. The yeast eats up some of the sugar. This creates bubbles.

The root beer is ready to be bottled! Once there are enough bubbles, the bottles are chilled. This stops the **yeast** from eating the sugar.

Brewers get to be creative when making root beer. There are so many great flavors to try!

AVERY'S
BEVERAGES
Bergkoff
DIET ROOTBEER
HOSMER
Root Beer
Racinette
ROOT BEER
ROUTE BEER 66
SIOUX CITY
ROOT BEER
TRIPLE XXX
ROOT BEER
DAD'S
Old Fashioned
ROOT BEER
DRAFT
ROOT BEER
Mason's
AMERICANA
ROOT BEER
The Pop Shoppe
ROOTBEER
SODA
RACINETTE
Sparky's
FRESH DRAFT
ROOT BEER
BUNDABERG
ROOT BEER
12.7 FL OZ (375mL)
Dang!
Root Beer
CRATER LAKE
ROOT BEER
CANADIAN
ORIGINAL
Harvey & Vern's
OLDE FASHIONED
ROOT BEER
RACINETTE
Foxon Park
DRAFT STYLE
ROOT BEER
Root Beer
Bedford's
Root Beer
Beer
Root Beer
Root Beer
I Sentence
You to
Drink my
Root Beer!
Judge
ROOT
BEER
diet
BEER
Olde
BROOKLYN
THOMAS
KEMPER
Root Beer
LOW CALORIE
THOMAS
KEMPER
Root Beer
ROOT BEER
ROOT
BEER
Salted Caramel
ROOT BEER
Big
Ben's
Root Beer!
FIREMAN'S
Brew

More Facts

- August 6th is National Root Beer Float Day!

- A&W is the best-selling root beer in the United States.

- Sassafras was banned by the Food & Drug Administration in 1960. Lab tests showed that it caused cancer. Today's root beer often has man-made sassafras flavoring.

Glossary

brewer – a person who makes root beer.

extract – a strong, concentrated substance.

filter – to go through a filter so that solids can be removed from a liquid.

pharmacist – a person who is trained to prepare and sell medicine.

root tea – a beverage made by steeping the roots of plants.

steep – to soak in a liquid.

yeast – tiny, single cells of certain fungi that are used to make certain foods and drinks.

Index

Abdo Kids ONLINE

FREE! ONLINE MULTIMEDIA RESOURCES

Visit abdokids.com and use this code to access crafts, games, videos, and more!